Civil Rights Crusaders

ROSA PARKS

By Barbara M. Linde

Gareth Stevens
Publishing

Please visit our website, www.garethstevens.com. For a free color catalog of all our high-quality books, call toll free 1-800-542-2595 or fax 1-877-542-2596.

Library of Congress Cataloging-in-Publication Data

Linde, Barbara M.
 Rosa Parks / Barbara M. Linde.
     p. cm. — (Civil rights crusaders)
 Includes index.
 ISBN 978-1-4339-5696-6 (pbk.)
 ISBN 978-1-4339-5697-3 (6-pack)
 ISBN 978-1-4339-5694-2 (library binding)
 1. Parks, Rosa, 1913-2005—Juvenile literature. 2. African American women—Alabama—Montgomery—Biography—Juvenile literature. 3. African Americans—Alabama—Montgomery—Biography—Juvenile literature. 4. Civil rights workers—Alabama—Montgomery—Biography—Juvenile literature. 5. African Americans—Civil rights—Alabama—Montgomery—History—20th century—Juvenile literature. 6. Segregation in transportation—Alabama—Montgomery—History—20th century—Juvenile literature. 7. Montgomery (Ala.)—Race relations—Juvenile literature. 8. Montgomery (Ala.)—Biography—Juvenile literature. I. Title.
 F334.M753P385535 2011
 323.092—dc22
 [B]
                                    2011010056

First Edition

Published in 2012 by
Gareth Stevens Publishing
111 East 14th Street, Suite 349
New York, NY 10003

Copyright © 2012 Gareth Stevens Publishing

Designer: Katelyn E. Reynolds
Editor: Kristen Rajczak

Photo credits: Cover, pp. 3–24, back cover (background) Shutterstock.com; cover, p. 1 Taro Yamasaki/Time & Life Pictures/Getty Images; p. 5 Paul Sancya/AFP/Getty Images; p. 7 Angel Franco/New York Times Co./Getty Images; p. 9 Robert Abbott Sengstacke/Getty Images; pp. 11, 13, 17 Don Cravens/Time & Life Pictures/Getty Images; p. 15 Grey Villet/Time & Life Pictures/Getty Images; p. 19 William Philpott/Getty Images.

All rights reserved. No part of this book may be reproduced in any form without permission in writing from the publisher, except by a reviewer.

Printed in the United States of America

CPSIA compliance information: Batch #CS11GS: For further information contact Gareth Stevens, New York, New York at 1-800-542-2595.

CONTENTS

Civil Rights Crusader 4

Early Life 6

Marriage and a Diploma 8

NAACP Secretary 10

"Tired of Giving In" 12

The Trial 14

The Montgomery Bus Boycott 16

Life in Detroit 18

The Crusade Goes On 20

Glossary 22

For More Information 23

Index 24

Words in the glossary appear in **bold** type the first time they are used in the text.

CIVIL RIGHTS CRUSADER

Rosa Parks was an important **civil rights** leader. She's often called the "mother" of the civil rights movement. Rosa fought **discrimination** for more than 50 years. She believed in using peaceful actions to make changes. Peace, justice, and equality for all were her goals.

Rosa once said, "I feel deeply that no human being should ever be treated unjustly. I am concerned about any discrimination, of any people." She **inspired** many people with her life and work.

Vice President Al Gore presents Rosa with the Congressional Gold Medal of Honor in 1999.

5

EARLY LIFE

Rosa Louise McCauley was born on February 4, 1913, in Tuskegee, Alabama. As a child, Rosa lived with her mother, younger brother, and grandparents in the small Alabama town of Pine Level, near Montgomery.

Rosa grew up knowing about racial discrimination. When Rosa was about 6, she started working in nearby cotton fields. She also went to **segregated** schools. Rosa was a good student and enjoyed learning. However, she had to leave school in the eleventh grade to take care of her sick grandmother and mother.

LET FREEDOM RING

Rosa's grandparents had been slaves. Her grandfather taught his children to stand up for themselves. Rosa's mother raised her children the same way.

Rosa attended many gatherings held in her honor throughout her life.

MARRIAGE AND A DIPLOMA

On December 18, 1932, Rosa married Raymond Parks. He wanted Rosa to finish high school. Not many black people graduated from high school at that time, but with her husband's help, Rosa did.

Raymond Parks was an **activist**. He was already a member of the **NAACP** when Rosa met him. He didn't want Rosa to join him. Going to NAACP meetings was very unsafe. Members might be arrested, hurt, or even killed if people who opposed civil rights for African Americans caught them.

LET FREEDOM RING

Segregation in public places was allowed because of the Jim Crow laws. These laws were in effect in the southern United States for almost a century—from the mid-1870s until the mid-1960s.

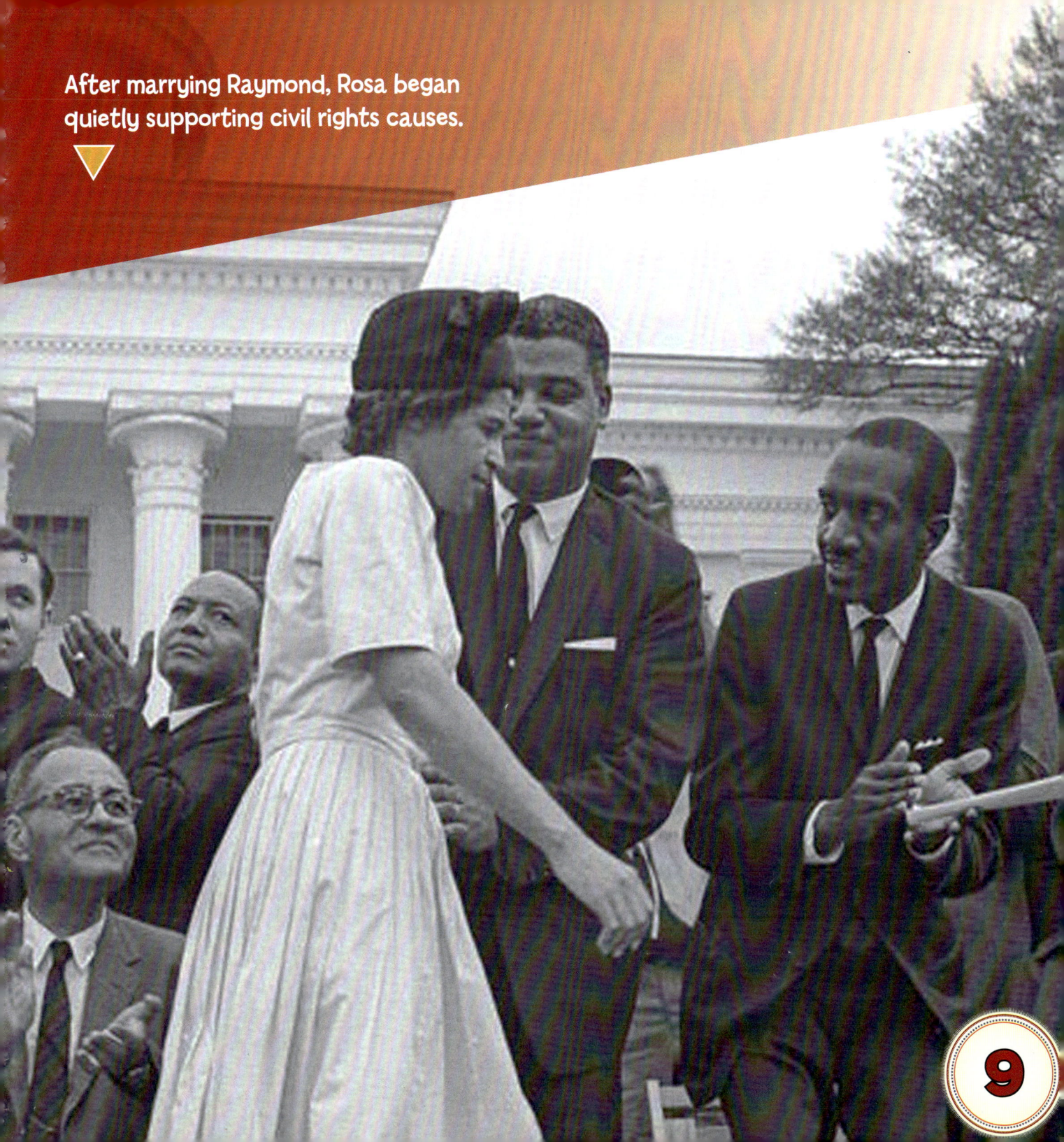

After marrying Raymond, Rosa began quietly supporting civil rights causes.

NAACP SECRETARY

In 1943, Rosa joined the Montgomery branch of the NAACP. She became secretary to the group's president, taking notes and keeping records. Rosa stayed in this position for more than 13 years. She also worked with the young people of the NAACP. All the while, she worked hard at a department store, too.

Rosa and other NAACP members supported justice and equality for black people. She said that they wanted to "let it be known that we did not wish to continue being second-class citizens."

LET FREEDOM RING

Rosa was also active in the Montgomery Voters League. Blacks had to pass a test so they could vote. The league helped them prepare for the test.

Rosa worked as a seamstress at the department store. It was her job to sew and mend clothes.

"TIRED OF GIVING IN"

After she left work on December 1, 1955, Rosa got on a bus in Montgomery and sat down in the middle section. Blacks were only allowed to sit there and in the back of the bus. At the next stop, the driver told Rosa and three other black riders to give up their seats for a white man. Rosa refused. The bus driver had her arrested, and the police took Rosa to jail.

Afterwards, Rosa said, "I was just tired of giving in."

LET FREEDOM RING

In 1943, a bus driver ordered Rosa off a bus because she got on at the front of the bus instead of the back like she was supposed to. That was the same driver who had her arrested in 1955.

Rosa's refusal to give up her seat became a very important moment in the civil rights movement.

THE TRIAL

Raymond and the NAACP leaders quickly got Rosa out of jail. She took her case to court. This would finally test the legality of segregation laws.

Black leaders organized a bus **boycott** in Montgomery the day of the trial. On December 5, 1955, blacks walked, carpooled, or took cabs to school or work. This was the first time the black community had **protested** as a group.

The local judge said Rosa was **guilty**. She was fined but not sent to jail. Rosa's lawyers asked a higher court to hear the case.

LET FREEDOM RING

Led by Martin Luther King Jr., black leaders formed the Montgomery Improvement Association (MIA) to organize and support the bus boycott.

Black workers walk to work during the bus boycott.

THE MONTGOMERY BUS BOYCOTT

The Montgomery Improvement Association continued the boycott. Blacks—and some whites—didn't ride public buses for 381 days. Rosa arranged rides for people and gave shoes to walkers. She visited other cities and states to tell groups about the boycott.

The bus company lost a lot of money. However, that wasn't enough to cause change. Many people disagreed with the boycott and even bullied MIA leaders.

At last, Rosa's case reached the **Supreme Court**. The court ruled that bus segregation was illegal. On December 20, 1956, the boycott ended.

LET FREEDOM RING

The Montgomery bus boycott was the beginning of the modern civil rights movement. Soon black groups in other cities organized bus boycotts and other peaceful protests.

Rosa and other blacks wait for the bus just a few days after the Supreme Court ruling in 1956.

Rosa Parks

31 DAYS SINCE TRAFFIC DEATH
Let's keep the light green!
MONTGOMERY JAYCEES

17

LIFE IN DETROIT

Rosa and Raymond soon moved to Detroit, Michigan. From 1965 to 1988, Rosa worked for an African American congressman, John Conyers. Rosa also continued to travel and talk about civil rights.

In 1987, Rosa and Elaine Steele founded the Rosa and Raymond Parks Institute for Self Development. The institute helps young people stay in school and make a difference in their communities. A summer program called Pathways to Freedom teaches students about the struggle for civil rights.

LET FREEDOM RING

In 1997, Michigan began celebrating Rosa Parks Day on the first Monday after February 4 every year.

Rosa made civil rights for all a lifelong goal. ▽

THE CRUSADE GOES ON

Rosa received many honors before her death in 2005. The NAACP and other groups gave her awards. The US government awarded her the Presidential Medal of Freedom and the Congressional Gold Medal of Honor. In 2002, there was a TV movie about her life.

Rosa Parks died on October 24, 2005. Her casket was placed in the US Capitol building on October 30. She was the first woman and second black American to be laid "in honor" in the Capitol. This is a recognition usually reserved for US government officials.

TIMELINE

1913 — Rosa Louise McCauley is born on February 4.

1932 — Rosa marries Raymond Parks.

1943 — Rosa joins the NAACP.

1955 — Rosa refuses to give up her seat on the bus on December 1. The Montgomery bus boycott begins on December 5.

1956 — The Supreme Court rules bus segregation illegal. The Montgomery bus boycott ends on December 20.

1957 — Rosa and Raymond move to Detroit, Michigan.

1987 — Rosa helps found the Rosa and Raymond Parks Institute for Self Development.

2005 — Rosa Parks dies on October 24.

GLOSSARY

activist: a person who works for a cause

boycott: the act of refusing to have dealings with a person or business in order to force change

civil rights: the freedoms granted to us by law

discrimination: treating people differently because of race or beliefs

guilty: at fault

inspire: to cause someone to want to do something

NAACP: the National Association for the Advancement of Colored People, a civil rights organization founded in 1909

protest: to object strongly to something. Also, an event at which a group objects to an idea, act, or way of doing something.

segregate: to forcibly separate races or classes

Supreme Court: the highest court in the United States

FOR MORE INFORMATION

Books

Fradin, Dennis Brindell. *The Montgomery Bus Boycott.* New York, NY: Marshall Cavendish Benchmark, 2010.

Gosman, Gillian. *Rosa Parks.* New York, NY: PowerKids Press, 2011.

Kittinger, Jo S. *Rosa's Bus.* Honesdale, PA: Calkins Creek, 2010.

Websites

Rosa & Raymond Parks Institute for Self Development
www.rosaparks.org
Read about the organization Rosa Parks helped found.

Stand Up for Your Rights
pbskids.org/wayback/civilrights
Learn more about your civil rights and the people who fought for them.

Publisher's note to educators and parents: Our editors have carefully reviewed these websites to ensure that they are suitable for students. Many websites change frequently, however, and we cannot guarantee that a site's future contents will continue to meet our high standards of quality and educational value. Be advised that students should be closely supervised whenever they access the Internet.

INDEX

awards 20
bus boycott 14, 15, 16, 21
Congressional Gold Medal of Honor 5, 20
Conyers, John 18
Detroit, Michigan 18, 21
discrimination 4, 6
equality 4, 10
grandparents 6
Jim Crow laws 8
justice 4, 10
King, Martin Luther, Jr. 14
McCauley, Rosa Louise 6, 21
Montgomery 6, 10, 12, 14, 16, 21
Montgomery Improvement Association 14, 16
Montgomery Voters League 10
"mother" of the civil rights movement 4
NAACP 8, 10, 14, 20, 21
Parks, Raymond 8, 9, 14, 18, 21
Pathways to Freedom 18
peace 4, 16
Pine Level 6
Presidential Medal of Freedom 20
Rosa and Raymond Parks Institute for Self Development 18, 21
Rosa Parks Day 18
segregation 6, 8, 14, 16, 21
slaves 6
Steele, Elaine 18
Supreme Court 16, 17, 21
Tuskegee, Alabama 6
TV movie 20
US Capitol 20

B P252L   HVINX
Linde, Barbara M.
Rosa Parks /

VINSON
07/12